HUMOR
Fuel That Keeps Us Going

L.E. Walsh

All Rights Reserved Copyright © 2018 by L.E. Walsh
This book or any portion thereof may not be reproduced or used in any manner whatsoever without the express written permission of the publisher except for the use of brief quotations in a book review.
Printed in the United States of America
First Printing, 2018
ISBN 978-1-7326169-4-3
Thirteen Stories Publishing
36500 Ford Road #156
Westland, MI 48185
thirteenstoriespublishing.com

To Christa, Heather and Nina who always make me laugh, and to all those who line my life's path with their smiles, *thank you*.

Preface

If at first you don't succeed,
that's to be expected.
(Courtesy of Thomas K. Walsh)

To My Editor,

    The Ultimate Revision:

        A Headstone.

CONTENTS

Chapter 1 – Common Sense Humor…1

Chapter 2 – Political Humor…22

Chapter 3 – Thinker's Humor…40

Chapter 4 – Sarcastic / Cynical Humor…60

Chapter 5 – Provocative Humor…72

The sticky stuff on envelopes should taste better.

Why do they call it "**bulk** mail"?
Just ask my garbage man.

If looking to the past were preferable,

our eyes

would be in the back of our heads.

Even bullshit mildews.

For some people,

extra-strength bathroom tissue is inadequate.

THE WALSH LAW OF DIMINISHING RETURNS:

As I approach middle-age, my standards

for a mate are less than

half what they

used to

be

.

Those who say

"clothes don't make the man"

ought to see one naked.

When *writing* a love letter,

breath mints don't help.

For a society focused on Characters,

Hollywood destroys many.

Definition of "historian":

    an advocate for hysterical hindsight.

Lethargy

and

fatigue,

So similar in symptoms, opposite in source.

If all men were bald,

barbers would have to look for work.

Speaking extemporaneously is like c

                                                  l

                                                  i

                                                  f

                                                      f

                                                          diving.

THE ABILITY TO REASON IS A TWO-EDGED SWORD.

ASK ANY MARRIED MAN.

For some people,

passing gas

is an *art form*.

A bird in the hand

better peck lightly.

If life really were a barrel of laughs, mine would be going over Niagara Falls.

The single,
most important key
to living to a ripe old age:

Longevity.

The best way to tie a knot is to be in a hurry.

1ˢᵗ Rule of Farming:

Never bale hay in the buff.

I wish politicians were as good as they think they are.

No wonder economics is so confusing.

Politicians keep promising Americans

a BigMac in every garage.

Politicians believe

all of society's ills can be resolved

by reinventing the wheel.

The elect should be called "poly-Titians"

    because of their plastic personalities.

        and all the fat.

If you must take the bull by the horns,

first make sure you have the right end of the bull.

Respect has nothing to do with *fear*,

everything to do with *truth*.

We give too much credit to those who do nothing.

Even those bent on cleaning up politics

can get dirty

Recurring government reports cover up economic realities like a homeowner applying paint over old, peeling layers.

Politics is not a profession

    even though the elect

        are paid for their votes.

Our Founding Fathers recognized
what was good for the country was good for them.

Modern-day leaders believe
what is good for them is good for the country.

Arrogance has no place among elected officials;

though it seems to have found comfortable surroundings,

nonetheless.

Our nation
      would be well-served
           to recognize that

         cartoon characters
              and
           politicians

are created pretty much
      the same way,

           by someone else.

Handling what politicians dish out is easier

when you already have shoveled out

several loads of the real stuff by ✋

To clean out our federal government completely would require a suppository the size of the Washington Monument.

thinker's humor

The ultimate success:

getting out of life alive.

Carry your own ammunition.

Even a leaky boat floats
                                    f
                                       o
                                          r
                                             a
                                                w
                                                 h
                                                 i
                                                 l
                                               e.

Hopelessness:

A man without a dream.

BOREDOM: the greatest killer of all time.

"Life as we know it,"

doesn't exist.

Humor:

God's aspirin for Earth's headaches.

Like clouds,

a marriage will disappear

with the addition of enough hot air.

Sometimes the obvious **IIS**.

Sometimes the **OBVIOUS** isint.

Quitting in the face of adversity

is like drinking to cover up your problems.

If all the wrapping paper in the world was laid

endlIdne,

I still wouldn't find that one present I lost in it.

Who was the first person ever to have

an acciden while wearing t\o/r\n underwear?
              t

Boredom results from eliminating ~~all~~ choices.

Fear strikes the untalented

    when exposed to the light of genius.

Age is life's ULTIMATE condiment.

FOREVER

is a good place to start.

WHY DOES A WOMAN CALL HER HAIR TREATMENT

a "permanent"

WHEN IT ISN'T?

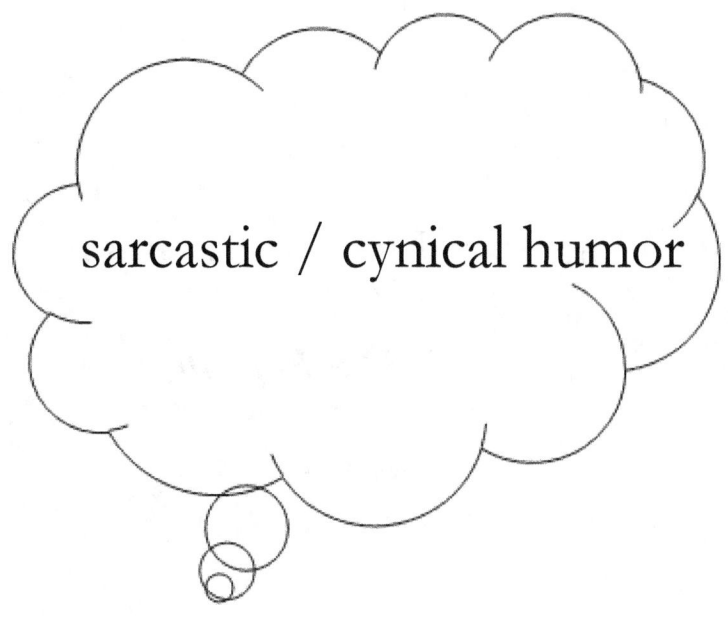

The State Flower of Pennsylvania:

The Pothole

(Quakus Infernus)

For those with insufficient tension in life:

stand on only one good leg and chop wood.

every smoker quits s
o
o
n
e
r
o
r
l
a
t
e
r

The ultimate **square peg** in a ROUND HOLE:

A calendar

There should be **ANOTHER NAME** for a Thesaurus.

Anybody who believes America is moving to a paperless society has never seen my office.

Snow is God's wrapping paper;

when removed,

the gift of spring is revealed.

With all the ringing in my ears,

Why can't I carry a tune?

Noticed the air freshener in the bathroom is marked "INSTITUTIONAL SIZE".

Is that saying something about where I am? Or should be?

Judging from the number of ballpoint pens in the desk, they figured out how to **ma te** .

Marriage is a fence that keeps

some people in

        and

                some out.

                        But nobody can sit on it.

children   easily
       a
        r
         e
       too

w   t
  r   h
    oug

(children are too easily wrought.)

The District of Columbia's State Bird:

The Naked-Breasted Middle Finger.

Lovers discussing permanent birth control:

"A stitch in mine saves thine".

Too bad so many people

consider life

a shitty first draft.

Instead of a woman, maybe I should marry one of my dogs.

The later I come home, the happier they are to see me.

We might be more respectful of ourselves IF,

on every anniversary of our birth, . . .

. . . each of us had to be photographed naked.

Does a cork *screw*?

NOTHING DISRUPTS LIFE AS MUCH AS LIVING TOGETHER.

Recovering from a divorce is like getting over the flu.

You've been miserable so long,
It takes a while to realize you feel fine.

The end of the book,
but not of humor.

Epilogue

When all else fails,
it figures.

www.ingramcontent.com/pod-product-compliance
Lightning Source LLC
Chambersburg PA
CBHW052107070526
44584CB00017B/2381